SCHOLASTIC INC.

EVERY TIME YOU READ THIS BOOK,
DRAW ANOTHER X IN THE RECTANGLE!

ISBN 978-1-338-54688-0

12 11 10 9 8 7 6 5 4 3 2 1   19 20 21 22 23 24

Printed in the U.S.A.

First Scholastic printing, January 2019

4

I'VE NEVER SEEN anyone ride so SLOWLY.

Yeah! Check it OUT!

Johnny Boo is an AWESOME Skateboarder.

I bet he knows a million cool tricks like that.

Z

Actually... I think he's asleep.

What? That's a silly skateboard trick.

Let's wake him up!

I'll tickle his foot.

Hello?! Are we there yet?

Tee hee

Is this the moon?

No, Johnny Boo.

It's a SKATEBOARD!

Oh.

You were doing a sleepy skateboard trick~

- so we woke you up!

YAWN

Hey!

NO YAWNING!

Night is no time to be a silly SLEEPYHEAD!

It's time to PLAY with us, Johnny Boo!

Sorry, guys.

I guess I fell asleep riding my skateboard to the MOON.

But you'll NEVER get there with those silly CIRCLE wheels.

I won't?

No WAY, Johnny Boo.

Z

CHAPTER THREE

Okay. A skateboard has **FOUR** wheels, so we'll need four stars.

Right!

Let's ask some friends to help.

Z

Do you guys want to help us help Johnny Boo?

Yes. That sounds fun!

We like to help!

Good.

Are there four of us now?

I think so!

Let's start helping!

We better count ourselves first, just to be sure.

Okay!

One. Two! Three!

Doggy!

Doggy is NOT a NUMBER!

Maybe it is.

How many legs does a doggy have?

Eleven? FOUR!

Okay. So I guess there ARE four of us.

Goody!

That means WE'RE READY!

We're Ready to help NOW, JOHNNY Boo. Hold up YOUR skateboard.

I don't know about this, guys... aren't wheels ROUND for a REASON?

Nope.

Nuh-uh.

No REASON.

None that I KNOW of.

No... I'm PRETTY SURE that ROUND wheels ROLL better.

That's NOT TRUE!

STARS are the COOLEST.

Fine.

I'll just show you. PROMISE you won't get all disappointedy and CRY-ish.

We PROMISE, Johnny Boo!

Well...

See what I mean? We're NOT ROLLING, are we?

I told you so.

Z

Well, Johnny Boo... if you're SO bored, maybe you should try doing some cool Skateboard tricks!

Yeah!

Do a trick!

Okay, watch this.

I'll do a Super ONE-footy.

Ta-da!

BORING.

Not cool enough.

Well... what SHOULD I do? An electric wiggle worm? A Boston Baked Bouncing Bean? A tubular toothpaste tumble-butt?

A front-row slider with a tornado twister backwards upsideways-down nuclear elbow felbow welbow shmelbow?

30

THE END!

**A PHOTO OF
THE AUTHOR AT WORK:**